ROMANCE BOOK

READING JOURNAL

SHE READS ROMANCE BOOKS

Created by
She Reads Romance Books

Where You'll Find:

- Epic Book Lists
- New Book Releases
- Annual Reading Challenge
- Romance Book Reading Journal
- Quizzes
- Honest Book Reviews

shereadsromancebooks.com

/shereadsromancebooks

/shereadsromancebooks

Visit Today!

THIS JOURNAL
BELONGS TO:

_____

My Reading Goals

Set an annual or monthly reading goals
and track your progress

My Reading Goal This Year:

_____ Books

January: _____ ☐

February: _____ ☐

March: _____ ☐

April: _____ ☐

May: _____ ☐

June: _____ ☐

July: _____ ☐

August: _____ ☐

September: _____ ☐

October: _____ ☐

November: _____ ☐

December: _____ ☐

Daily Reading Tracker

YEAR: _____

	JAN	FEB	MAR	APR	MAY	JUN	JUL	AUG	SEP	OCT	NOV	DEC
1	☐	☐	☐	☐	☐	☐	☐	☐	☐	☐	☐	☐
2	☐	☐	☐	☐	☐	☐	☐	☐	☐	☐	☐	☐
3	☐	☐	☐	☐	☐	☐	☐	☐	☐	☐	☐	☐
4	☐	☐	☐	☐	☐	☐	☐	☐	☐	☐	☐	☐
5	☐	☐	☐	☐	☐	☐	☐	☐	☐	☐	☐	☐
6	☐	☐	☐	☐	☐	☐	☐	☐	☐	☐	☐	☐
7	☐	☐	☐	☐	☐	☐	☐	☐	☐	☐	☐	☐
8	☐	☐	☐	☐	☐	☐	☐	☐	☐	☐	☐	☐
9	☐	☐	☐	☐	☐	☐	☐	☐	☐	☐	☐	☐
10	☐	☐	☐	☐	☐	☐	☐	☐	☐	☐	☐	☐
11	☐	☐	☐	☐	☐	☐	☐	☐	☐	☐	☐	☐
12	☐	☐	☐	☐	☐	☐	☐	☐	☐	☐	☐	☐
13	☐	☐	☐	☐	☐	☐	☐	☐	☐	☐	☐	☐
14	☐	☐	☐	☐	☐	☐	☐	☐	☐	☐	☐	☐
15	☐	☐	☐	☐	☐	☐	☐	☐	☐	☐	☐	☐
16	☐	☐	☐	☐	☐	☐	☐	☐	☐	☐	☐	☐
17	☐	☐	☐	☐	☐	☐	☐	☐	☐	☐	☐	☐
18	☐	☐	☐	☐	☐	☐	☐	☐	☐	☐	☐	☐
19	☐	☐	☐	☐	☐	☐	☐	☐	☐	☐	☐	☐
20	☐	☐	☐	☐	☐	☐	☐	☐	☐	☐	☐	☐
21	☐	☐	☐	☐	☐	☐	☐	☐	☐	☐	☐	☐
22	☐	☐	☐	☐	☐	☐	☐	☐	☐	☐	☐	☐
23	☐	☐	☐	☐	☐	☐	☐	☐	☐	☐	☐	☐
24	☐	☐	☐	☐	☐	☐	☐	☐	☐	☐	☐	☐
25	☐	☐	☐	☐	☐	☐	☐	☐	☐	☐	☐	☐
26	☐	☐	☐	☐	☐	☐	☐	☐	☐	☐	☐	☐
27	☐	☐	☐	☐	☐	☐	☐	☐	☐	☐	☐	☐
28	☐	☐	☐	☐	☐	☐	☐	☐	☐	☐	☐	☐
29	☐	☐	☐	☐	☐	☐	☐	☐	☐	☐	☐	☐
30	☐		☐	☐	☐	☐	☐	☐	☐	☐	☐	☐
31	☐		☐		☐		☐	☐		☐		☐

Reading Challenge

Read 12 Books in One Year
From My Favorite Book Lists

- [ ] Enemies to Lovers Romance
- [ ] Friends to Lovers Romance
- [ ] Second Chance Romance
- [ ] Fake Relationship Romance
- [ ] Marriage of Convenience Romance
- [ ] Historical Romance
- [ ] Billionaire Romance
- [ ] Erotic Romance
- [ ] College Romance
- [ ] Office Romance
- [ ] Sports Romance
- [ ] Fantasy Romance

Romance Trope Bingo

Second Chance	Tortured Hero	Fake Relationship	Taboo Relationship	Single Parent
Left at the Altar	Teacher Student	Shape Shifter	Enemies to Lovers	Royal Romance
Love Triangle	Surprise Pregnancy	FREE	Modern Retelling	Forced Proximity
Neighbors to Lovers	Rock Star Romance	Best Friend's Sibling	Strong Heroine	Marriage of Convenience
Nanny Romance	Friends to Lovers	Small Town Romance	Slow Burn	Office Romance

My Bookshelf

Write in the Books on Your Bookshelf

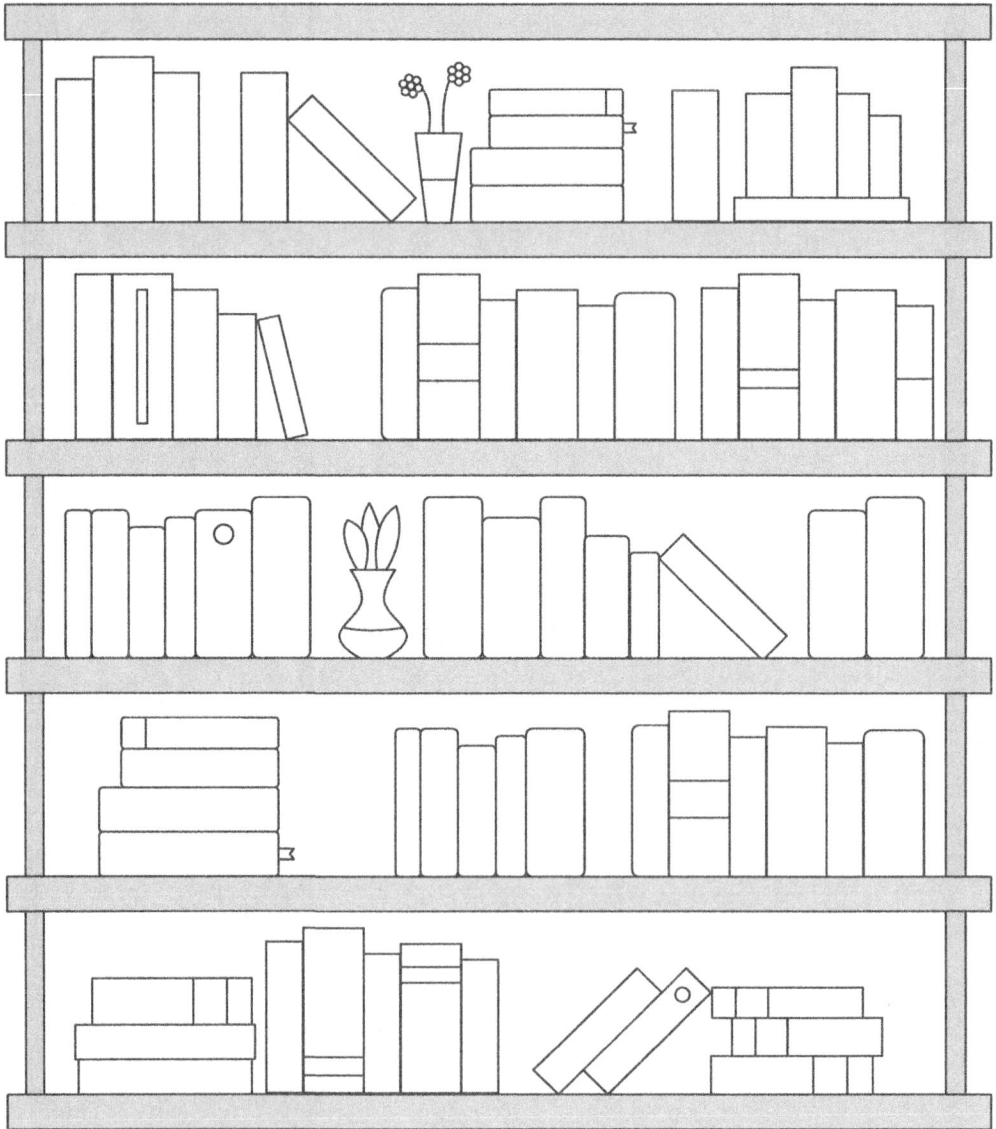

To Read List:

Title	Author	Read
		☐
		☐
		☐
		☐
		☐
		☐
		☐
		☐
		☐
		☐
		☐
		☐
		☐
		☐
		☐
		☐
		☐

To Read List:

Title	Author	Read
		☐
		☐
		☐
		☐
		☐
		☐
		☐
		☐
		☐
		☐
		☐
		☐
		☐
		☐
		☐
		☐
		☐

To Read List:

Title	Author	Read
		☐
		☐
		☐
		☐
		☐
		☐
		☐
		☐
		☐
		☐
		☐
		☐
		☐
		☐
		☐
		☐
		☐
		☐

To Read List:

Title	Author	Read
		☐
		☐
		☐
		☐
		☐
		☐
		☐
		☐
		☐
		☐
		☐
		☐
		☐
		☐
		☐
		☐
		☐

Favorites

Favorite Books

Title: _____ Author: _____

what I loved...

Title: _____ Author: _____

what I loved...

Title: _____ Author: _____

what I loved...

Title: _____ Author: _____

what I loved...

Title: _____ Author: _____

what I loved...

Favorite Books

Title: _____ Author: _____

```
┌──────────────────────────────────────────────────────────┐
│ what I loved...                                            │
│                                                            │
│                                                            │
└──────────────────────────────────────────────────────────┘
```

Title: _____ Author: _____

```
┌──────────────────────────────────────────────────────────┐
│ what I loved...                                            │
│                                                            │
│                                                            │
└──────────────────────────────────────────────────────────┘
```

Title: _____ Author: _____

```
┌──────────────────────────────────────────────────────────┐
│ what I loved...                                            │
│                                                            │
│                                                            │
└──────────────────────────────────────────────────────────┘
```

Title: _____ Author: _____

```
┌──────────────────────────────────────────────────────────┐
│ what I loved...                                            │
│                                                            │
│                                                            │
└──────────────────────────────────────────────────────────┘
```

Title: _____ Author: _____

```
┌──────────────────────────────────────────────────────────┐
│ what I loved...                                            │
│                                                            │
│                                                            │
└──────────────────────────────────────────────────────────┘
```

Favorite Books

Title: _____   Author: _____

what I loved...

Title: _____   Author: _____

what I loved...

Title: _____   Author: _____

what I loved...

Title: _____   Author: _____

what I loved...

Title: _____   Author: _____

what I loved...

Favorite Books

Title: _____ Author: _____

> *what I loved...*

Title: _____ Author: _____

> *what I loved...*

Title: _____ Author: _____

> *what I loved...*

Title: _____ Author: _____

> *what I loved...*

Title: _____ Author: _____

> *what I loved...*

Five Star Books

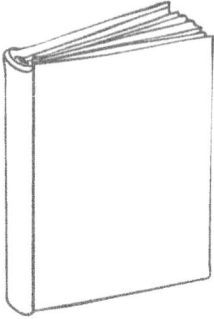

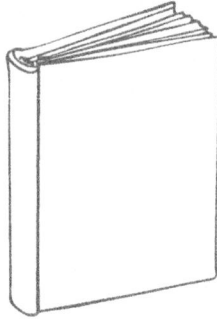

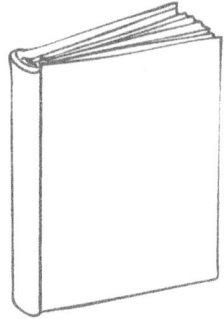

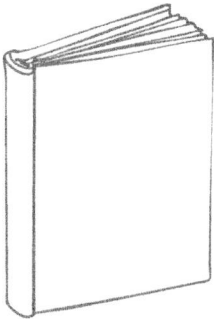

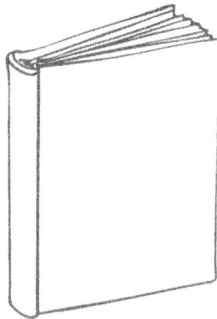

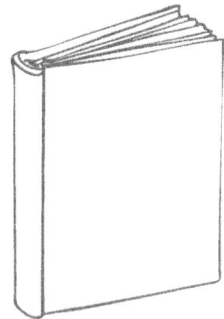

★ ★ ★ ★ ★

_____
_____
_____

★ ★ ★ ★ ★

_____
_____
_____

★ ★ ★ ★ ★

_____
_____
_____

★ ★ ★ ★ ★

_____
_____
_____

★ ★ ★ ★ ★

_____
_____
_____

★ ★ ★ ★ ★

_____
_____
_____

Five Star Books

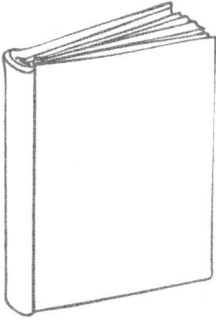

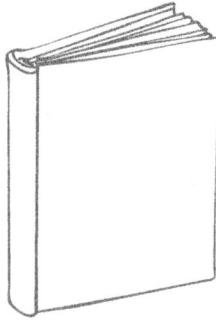

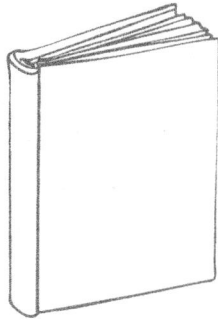

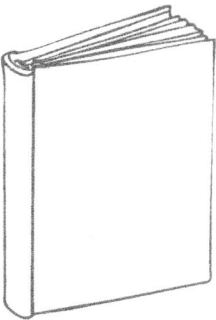

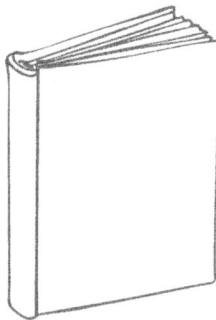

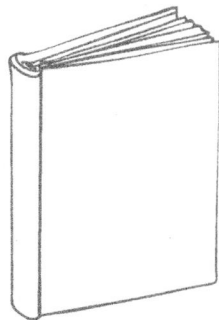

Favorite Book Boyfriends

Character:

Title: _____ Author: _____

what I loved...

Character:

Title: _____ Author: _____

what I loved...

Character:

Title: _____ Author: _____

what I loved...

Character:

Title: _____ Author: _____

what I loved...

Favorite Book Boyfriends

Character:

Title: Author:

what I loved...

Character:

Title: Author:

what I loved...

Character:

Title: Author:

what I loved...

Character:

Title: Author:

what I loved...

Favorite Book Boyfriends

Character:

Title: Author:

what I loved...

Character:

Title: Author:

what I loved...

Character:

Title: Author:

what I loved...

Character:

Title: Author:

what I loved...

Favorite Authors

Favorite Quotes

Title:

> 66
>
> Page:

Title:

> 66
>
> Page:

Title:

> 66
>
> Page:

Title:

> 66
>
> Page:

Title:

> 66
>
> Page:

Title:

> 66
>
> Page:

Title:

> 66
>
> Page:

Title:

> 66
>
> Page:

Favorite Quotes

Title: _____

> 66

Page:

Title: _____

> 66

Page:

Title: _____

> 66

Page:

Title: _____

> 66

Page:

Title: _____

> 66

Page:

Title: _____

> 66

Page:

Title: _____

> 66

Page:

Title: _____

> 66

Page:

Favorite Quotes

Title: _____

> 66

Page: _____

Title: _____

> 66

Page: _____

Title: _____

> 66

Page: _____

Title: _____

> 66

Page: _____

Title: _____

> 66

Page: _____

Title: _____

> 66

Page: _____

Title: _____

> 66

Page: _____

Title: _____

> 66

Page: _____

Book
Reviews

Book Review

Title: _____ Author: _____

Published Date: _____ Series: _____

Category: _____ Trope: _____

Date Read: _____ Themes: _____

Rating: ⭐ ⭐ ⭐ ⭐ ⭐ Characters: _____

Steam Level: 🌶 🌶 🌶 🌶 🌶 Book Type: Book | Ebook | Audio

Recommend: Y ☐ N ☐ To: _____

Summary

What I Loved

Quotes to Keep

66

99

Book Review

Title: _____   Author: _____

Published Date: _____   Series: _____

Category: _____   Trope: _____

Date Read: _____   Themes: _____

Rating: ⭐ ⭐ ⭐ ⭐ ⭐   Characters: _____

Steam Level: 🌶 🌶 🌶 🌶 🌶   Book Type: Book | Ebook | Audio

Recommend: Y ☐   N ☐   To: _____

Summary

What I Loved

Quotes to Keep

66

99

Book Review

Title: _____   Author: _____

Published Date: _____   Series: _____

Category: _____   Trope: _____

Date Read: _____   Themes: _____

Rating: ⭐ ⭐ ⭐ ⭐ ⭐   Characters: _____

Steam Level: 🌶 🌶 🌶 🌶 🌶   Book Type: Book | Ebook | Audio

Recommend: Y ☐ N ☐ To: _____

Summary

What I Loved

Quotes to Keep

66

99

Book Review

Title: _____ Author: _____

Published Date: _____ Series: _____

Category: _____ Trope: _____

Date Read: _____ Themes: _____

Rating: ⭐ ⭐ ⭐ ⭐ ⭐ Characters: _____

Steam Level: 🌶 🌶 🌶 🌶 🌶 Book Type: Book | Ebook | Audio

Recommend: Y ☐ N ☐ To: _____

Summary

What I Loved

Quotes to Keep

66

99

Book Review

Title: _____ Author: _____

Published Date: _____ Series: _____

Category: _____ Trope: _____

Date Read: _____ Themes: _____

Rating: ⭐ ⭐ ⭐ ⭐ ⭐ Characters: _____

Steam Level: 🌶 🌶 🌶 🌶 🌶 Book Type: Book | Ebook | Audio

Recommend: Y ☐ N ☐ To: _____

Summary

What I Loved

Quotes to Keep

66

99

Book Review

Title: _____   Author: _____

Published Date: _____   Series: _____

Category: _____   Trope: _____

Date Read: _____   Themes: _____

Rating: ⭐ ⭐ ⭐ ⭐ ⭐   Characters: _____

Steam Level: 🌶 🌶 🌶 🌶 🌶   Book Type: Book | Ebook | Audio

Recommend: Y ☐   N ☐   To: _____

Summary

What I Loved

Quotes to Keep

" "

Book Review

Title: _____   Author: _____

Published Date: _____   Series: _____

Category: _____   Trope: _____

Date Read: _____   Themes: _____

Rating: ★ ★ ★ ★ ★   Characters: _____

Steam Level: 🌶 🌶 🌶 🌶 🌶   Book Type: Book | Ebook | Audio

Recommend: Y ☐ N ☐ To: _____

Summary

What I Loved

Quotes to Keep
66 ... 99

Book Review

Title: _____   Author: _____

Published Date: _____   Series: _____

Category: _____   Trope: _____

Date Read: _____   Themes: _____

Rating: ⭐ ⭐ ⭐ ⭐ ⭐   Characters: _____

Steam Level: 🌶️ 🌶️ 🌶️ 🌶️ 🌶️   Book Type: Book | Ebook | Audio

Recommend: Y ☐   N ☐   To: _____

Summary

What I Loved

Quotes to Keep

66

99

Book Review

Title: _____ Author: _____

Published Date: _____ Series: _____

Category: _____ Trope: _____

Date Read: _____ Themes: _____

Rating: ⭐ ⭐ ⭐ ⭐ ⭐ Characters: _____

Steam Level: 🌶 🌶 🌶 🌶 🌶 Book Type: Book | Ebook | Audio

Recommend: Y ☐ N ☐ To: _____

Summary

What I Loved

Quotes to Keep

"

"

Book Review

Title: _____   Author: _____

Published Date: _____   Series: _____

Category: _____   Trope: _____

Date Read: _____   Themes: _____

Rating: ⭐ ⭐ ⭐ ⭐ ⭐   Characters: _____

Steam Level: 🌶 🌶 🌶 🌶 🌶   Book Type: Book | Ebook | Audio

Recommend: Y ☐   N ☐   To: _____

Summary

What I Loved

Quotes to Keep

66

99

Book Review

Title: _____   Author: _____

Published Date: _____   Series: _____

Category: _____   Trope: _____

Date Read: _____   Themes: _____

Rating: ⭐ ⭐ ⭐ ⭐ ⭐   Characters: _____

Steam Level: 🌶 🌶 🌶 🌶 🌶   Book Type: Book | Ebook | Audio

Recommend: Y ☐ N ☐ To: _____

Summary

What I Loved

Quotes to Keep

66

99

Book Review

Title: _____   Author: _____

Published Date: _____   Series: _____

Category: _____   Trope: _____

Date Read: _____   Themes: _____

Rating: ⭐ ⭐ ⭐ ⭐ ⭐   Characters: _____

Steam Level: 🌶 🌶 🌶 🌶 🌶   Book Type: Book | Ebook | Audio

Recommend: Y ☐ N ☐ To: _____

Summary

What I Loved

Quotes to Keep

"

"

Book Review

Title: _____   Author: _____

Published Date: _____   Series: _____

Category: _____   Trope: _____

Date Read: _____   Themes: _____

Rating: ⭐ ⭐ ⭐ ⭐ ⭐   Characters: _____

Steam Level: 🌶️ 🌶️ 🌶️ 🌶️ 🌶️   Book Type: Book | Ebook | Audio

Recommend: Y ☐ N ☐ To: _____

Summary

What I Loved

Quotes to Keep

" "

Book Review

Title: _____

Author: _____

Published Date: _____

Series: _____

Category: _____

Trope: _____

Date Read: _____

Themes: _____

Rating: ⭐ ⭐ ⭐ ⭐ ⭐

Characters: _____

Steam Level: 🌶 🌶 🌶 🌶 🌶

Book Type: Book | Ebook | Audio

Recommend: Y ☐   N ☐   To: _____

Summary

What I Loved

Quotes to Keep

66

99

Book Review

Title: _____ Author: _____

Published Date: _____ Series: _____

Category: _____ Trope: _____

Date Read: _____ Themes: _____

Rating: ⭐ ⭐ ⭐ ⭐ ⭐ Characters: _____

Steam Level: 🌶️ 🌶️ 🌶️ 🌶️ 🌶️ Book Type: Book | Ebook | Audio

Recommend: Y ☐ N ☐ To: _____

Summary

What I Loved

Quotes to Keep

"

"

Book Review

Title: _____ Author: _____

Published Date: _____ Series: _____

Category: _____ Trope: _____

Date Read: _____ Themes: _____

Rating: ⭐ ⭐ ⭐ ⭐ ⭐ Characters: _____

Steam Level: 🌶 🌶 🌶 🌶 🌶 Book Type: Book | Ebook | Audio

Recommend: Y ☐ N ☐ To: _____

Summary

What I Loved

Quotes to Keep

66

99

Book Review

Title: _____ Author: _____

Published Date: _____ Series: _____

Category: _____ Trope: _____

Date Read: _____ Themes: _____

Rating: ⭐ ⭐ ⭐ ⭐ ⭐ Characters: _____

Steam Level: 🌶 🌶 🌶 🌶 🌶 Book Type: Book | Ebook | Audio

Recommend: Y ☐ N ☐ To: _____

Summary

What I Loved

Quotes to Keep

66

99

Book Review

Title: _____

Author: _____

Published Date: _____

Series: _____

Category: _____

Trope: _____

Date Read: _____

Themes: _____

Rating: ⭐ ⭐ ⭐ ⭐ ⭐

Characters: _____

Steam Level: 🌶 🌶 🌶 🌶 🌶

Book Type: Book | Ebook | Audio

Recommend: Y ☐   N ☐   To: _____

Summary

What I Loved

Quotes to Keep

"

"

Book Review

Title: _____   Author: _____

Published Date: _____   Series: _____

Category: _____   Trope: _____

Date Read: _____   Themes: _____

Rating: ⭐ ⭐ ⭐ ⭐ ⭐   Characters: _____

Steam Level: 🌶 🌶 🌶 🌶 🌶   Book Type: Book | Ebook | Audio

Recommend: Y ☐   N ☐   To: _____

Summary

What I Loved

Quotes to Keep

"

"

Book Review

Title: _____   Author: _____

Published Date: _____   Series: _____

Category: _____   Trope: _____

Date Read: _____   Themes: _____

Rating: ⭐ ⭐ ⭐ ⭐ ⭐   Characters: _____

Steam Level: 🌶 🌶 🌶 🌶 🌶   Book Type: Book | Ebook | Audio

Recommend: Y ☐   N ☐   To: _____

Summary

What I Loved

Quotes to Keep

66

99

Book Review

Title: _____   Author: _____

Published Date: _____   Series: _____

Category: _____   Trope: _____

Date Read: _____   Themes: _____

Rating: ⭐ ⭐ ⭐ ⭐ ⭐   Characters: _____

Steam Level: 🌶 🌶 🌶 🌶 🌶   Book Type: Book | Ebook | Audio

Recommend: Y ☐   N ☐   To: _____

Summary

What I Loved

Quotes to Keep

66

99

Book Review

Title: _____   Author: _____

Published Date: _____   Series: _____

Category: _____   Trope: _____

Date Read: _____   Themes: _____

Rating: ⭐ ⭐ ⭐ ⭐ ⭐   Characters: _____

Steam Level: 🌶 🌶 🌶 🌶 🌶   Book Type: Book | Ebook | Audio

Recommend: Y ☐   N ☐   To: _____

Summary

What I Loved

Quotes to Keep

66

99

Book Review

Title: _____   Author: _____

Published Date: _____   Series: _____

Category: _____   Trope: _____

Date Read: _____   Themes: _____

Rating: ⭐ ⭐ ⭐ ⭐ ⭐   Characters: _____

Steam Level: 🌶 🌶 🌶 🌶 🌶   Book Type: Book | Ebook | Audio

Recommend: Y ☐   N ☐   To: _____

Summary

What I Loved

Quotes to Keep

66

99

Book Review

Title: _____ Author: _____

Published Date: _____ Series: _____

Category: _____ Trope: _____

Date Read: _____ Themes: _____

Rating: ⭐ ⭐ ⭐ ⭐ ⭐ Characters: _____

Steam Level: 🌶 🌶 🌶 🌶 🌶 Book Type: Book | Ebook | Audio

Recommend: Y ☐ N ☐ To: _____

Summary

What I Loved

Quotes to Keep

66

99

Book Review

Title: _____   Author: _____

Published Date: _____   Series: _____

Category: _____   Trope: _____

Date Read: _____   Themes: _____

Rating: ⭐ ⭐ ⭐ ⭐ ⭐   Characters: _____

Steam Level: 🌶 🌶 🌶 🌶 🌶   Book Type: Book | Ebook | Audio

Recommend: Y ☐ N ☐ To: _____

Summary

What I Loved

Quotes to Keep

"

"

Book Review

Title: _____   Author: _____

Published Date: _____   Series: _____

Category: _____   Trope: _____

Date Read: _____   Themes: _____

Rating: ⭐ ⭐ ⭐ ⭐ ⭐   Characters: _____

Steam Level: 🌶 🌶 🌶 🌶 🌶   Book Type: Book | Ebook | Audio

Recommend: Y ☐   N ☐   To: _____

Summary

What I Loved

Quotes to Keep

66

99

Book Review

Title: _____ Author: _____

Published Date: _____ Series: _____

Category: _____ Trope: _____

Date Read: _____ Themes: _____

Rating: ⭐ ⭐ ⭐ ⭐ ⭐ Characters: _____

Steam Level: 🌶 🌶 🌶 🌶 🌶 Book Type: Book | Ebook | Audio

Recommend: Y ☐ N ☐ To: _____

Summary

What I Loved

Quotes to Keep

66

99

Book Review

Title: _____   Author: _____

Published Date: _____   Series: _____

Category: _____   Trope: _____

Date Read: _____   Themes: _____

Rating: ⭐ ⭐ ⭐ ⭐ ⭐   Characters: _____

Steam Level: 🌶 🌶 🌶 🌶 🌶   Book Type: Book | Ebook | Audio

Recommend: Y ☐   N ☐   To: _____

Summary

What I Loved

Quotes to Keep

66

99

Book Review

Title: _____   Author: _____

Published Date: _____   Series: _____

Category: _____   Trope: _____

Date Read: _____   Themes: _____

Rating: ⭐ ⭐ ⭐ ⭐ ⭐   Characters: _____

Steam Level: 🌶 🌶 🌶 🌶 🌶   Book Type: Book | Ebook | Audio

Recommend: Y ☐   N ☐   To: _____

Summary

What I Loved

Quotes to Keep

66

99

Book Review

Title: _____   Author: _____

Published Date: _____   Series: _____

Category: _____   Trope: _____

Date Read: _____   Themes: _____

Rating: ⭐ ⭐ ⭐ ⭐ ⭐   Characters: _____

Steam Level: 🌶️ 🌶️ 🌶️ 🌶️ 🌶️   Book Type: Book | Ebook | Audio

Recommend: Y ☐   N ☐   To: _____

Summary

What I Loved

Quotes to Keep

66

99

Book Review

Title: _____   Author: _____

Published Date: _____   Series: _____

Category: _____   Trope: _____

Date Read: _____   Themes: _____

Rating: ⭐ ⭐ ⭐ ⭐ ⭐   Characters: _____

Steam Level: 🌶 🌶 🌶 🌶 🌶   Book Type: Book | Ebook | Audio

Recommend: Y ☐ N ☐ To: _____

Summary

What I Loved

Quotes to Keep

66

99

Book Review

Title: _____

Author: _____

Published Date: _____

Series: _____

Category: _____

Trope: _____

Date Read: _____

Themes: _____

Rating: ★ ★ ★ ★ ★

Characters: _____

Steam Level: 🌶 🌶 🌶 🌶 🌶

Book Type: Book | Ebook | Audio

Recommend: Y ☐   N ☐   To: _____

Summary

What I Loved

Quotes to Keep

66

99

Book Review

Title: _____ Author: _____

Published Date: _____ Series: _____

Category: _____ Trope: _____

Date Read: _____ Themes: _____

Rating: ⭐ ⭐ ⭐ ⭐ ⭐   Characters: _____

Steam Level: 🌶 🌶 🌶 🌶 🌶   Book Type: Book | Ebook | Audio

Recommend: Y ☐ N ☐ To: _____

Summary

What I Loved

Quotes to Keep

66

99

Book Review

Title: _____ Author: _____

Published Date: _____ Series: _____

Category: _____ Trope: _____

Date Read: _____ Themes: _____

Rating: ⭐ ⭐ ⭐ ⭐ ⭐ Characters: _____

Steam Level: 🌶 🌶 🌶 🌶 🌶 Book Type: Book | Ebook | Audio

Recommend: Y ☐   N ☐   To: _____

Summary

What I Loved

Quotes to Keep

66

99

Book Review

Title: _____   Author: _____

Published Date: _____   Series: _____

Category: _____   Trope: _____

Date Read: _____   Themes: _____

Rating: ⭐ ⭐ ⭐ ⭐ ⭐   Characters: _____

Steam Level: 🌶 🌶 🌶 🌶 🌶   Book Type: Book | Ebook | Audio

Recommend: Y ☐   N ☐   To: _____

Summary

What I Loved

Quotes to Keep

66

99

Book Review

Title: _____   Author: _____

Published Date: _____   Series: _____

Category: _____   Trope: _____

Date Read: _____   Themes: _____

Rating: ★ ★ ★ ★ ★   Characters: _____

Steam Level: 🌶 🌶 🌶 🌶 🌶   Book Type: Book | Ebook | Audio

Recommend: Y ☐   N ☐   To: _____

Summary

What I Loved

Quotes to Keep

66

99

Book Review

Title: _____ Author: _____

Published Date: _____ Series: _____

Category: _____ Trope: _____

Date Read: _____ Themes: _____

Rating: ⭐ ⭐ ⭐ ⭐ ⭐ Characters: _____

Steam Level: 🌶 🌶 🌶 🌶 🌶 Book Type: Book | Ebook | Audio

Recommend: Y ☐ N ☐ To: _____

Summary

What I Loved

Quotes to Keep

66

99

Book Review

Title: _____   Author: _____

Published Date: _____   Series: _____

Category: _____   Trope: _____

Date Read: _____   Themes: _____

Rating: ⭐ ⭐ ⭐ ⭐ ⭐   Characters: _____

Steam Level: 🌶 🌶 🌶 🌶 🌶   Book Type: Book | Ebook | Audio

Recommend: Y ☐   N ☐   To: _____

Summary

What I Loved

Quotes to Keep

66

99

Book Review

Title: _____ Author: _____

Published Date: _____ Series: _____

Category: _____ Trope: _____

Date Read: _____ Themes: _____

Rating: ⭐ ⭐ ⭐ ⭐ ⭐ Characters: _____

Steam Level: 🌶 🌶 🌶 🌶 🌶 Book Type: Book | Ebook | Audio

Recommend: Y ☐ N ☐ To: _____

Summary

What I Loved

Quotes to Keep

" "

Book Review

Title: _____   Author: _____

Published Date: _____   Series: _____

Category: _____   Trope: _____

Date Read: _____   Themes: _____

Rating: ⭐ ⭐ ⭐ ⭐ ⭐   Characters: _____

Steam Level: 🌶 🌶 🌶 🌶 🌶   Book Type: Book | Ebook | Audio

Recommend: Y ☐   N ☐   To: _____

Summary

What I Loved

Quotes to Keep

"
"

Book Review

Title: _____   Author: _____

Published Date: _____   Series: _____

Category: _____   Trope: _____

Date Read: _____   Themes: _____

Rating: ⭐ ⭐ ⭐ ⭐ ⭐   Characters: _____

Steam Level: 🌶 🌶 🌶 🌶 🌶   Book Type: Book | Ebook | Audio

Recommend: Y ☐   N ☐   To: _____

Summary

What I Loved

Quotes to Keep

"

"

Book Review

Title: _____   Author: _____

Published Date: _____   Series: _____

Category: _____   Trope: _____

Date Read: _____   Themes: _____

Rating: ⭐ ⭐ ⭐ ⭐ ⭐   Characters: _____

Steam Level: 🌶 🌶 🌶 🌶 🌶   Book Type: Book | Ebook | Audio

Recommend: Y ☐ N ☐ To: _____

Summary

What I Loved

Quotes to Keep

"

"

Book Review

Title: _____ Author: _____

Published Date: _____ Series: _____

Category: _____ Trope: _____

Date Read: _____ Themes: _____

Rating: ⭐ ⭐ ⭐ ⭐ ⭐ Characters: _____

Steam Level: 🌶 🌶 🌶 🌶 🌶 Book Type: Book | Ebook | Audio

Recommend: Y ☐ N ☐ To: _____

Summary

What I Loved

Quotes to Keep

"

"

Book Review

Title: _____ Author: _____

Published Date: _____ Series: _____

Category: _____ Trope: _____

Date Read: _____ Themes: _____

Rating: ⭐ ⭐ ⭐ ⭐ ⭐ Characters: _____

Steam Level: 🌶 🌶 🌶 🌶 🌶 Book Type: Book | Ebook | Audio

Recommend: Y ☐ N ☐ To: _____

Summary

What I Loved

Quotes to Keep

66

99

Book Review

Title: _____ Author: _____

Published Date: _____ Series: _____

Category: _____ Trope: _____

Date Read: _____ Themes: _____

Rating: ⭐ ⭐ ⭐ ⭐ ⭐ Characters: _____

Steam Level: 🌶 🌶 🌶 🌶 🌶 Book Type: Book | Ebook | Audio

Recommend: Y ☐ N ☐ To: _____

What I Loved

Quotes to Keep

66

99

Book Review

Title: _____ Author: _____

Published Date: _____ Series: _____

Category: _____ Trope: _____

Date Read: _____ Themes: _____

Rating: ⭐ ⭐ ⭐ ⭐ ⭐ Characters: _____

Steam Level: 🌶 🌶 🌶 🌶 🌶 Book Type: Book | Ebook | Audio

Recommend: Y ☐ N ☐ To: _____

Summary

What I Loved

Quotes to Keep

" "

Book Review

Title: _____   Author: _____

Published Date: _____   Series: _____

Category: _____   Trope: _____

Date Read: _____   Themes: _____

Rating: ⭐ ⭐ ⭐ ⭐ ⭐   Characters: _____

Steam Level: 🌶 🌶 🌶 🌶 🌶   Book Type: Book | Ebook | Audio

Recommend: Y ☐   N ☐   To: _____

Summary

What I Loved

Quotes to Keep

66

99

Book Review

Title: _____ Author: _____

Published Date: _____ Series: _____

Category: _____ Trope: _____

Date Read: _____ Themes: _____

Rating: ⭐ ⭐ ⭐ ⭐ ⭐ Characters: _____

Steam Level: 🌶 🌶 🌶 🌶 🌶 Book Type: Book | Ebook | Audio

Recommend: Y ☐ N ☐ To: _____

Summary

What I Loved

Quotes to Keep

66

99

Book Review

Title: _____   Author: _____

Published Date: _____   Series: _____

Category: _____   Trope: _____

Date Read: _____   Themes: _____

Rating: ⭐ ⭐ ⭐ ⭐ ⭐   Characters: _____

Steam Level: 🌶 🌶 🌶 🌶 🌶   Book Type: Book | Ebook | Audio

Recommend: Y ☐ N ☐ To: _____

Summary

What I Loved

Quotes to Keep

"

"

Book Review

Title: _____ Author: _____

Published Date: _____ Series: _____

Category: _____ Trope: _____

Date Read: _____ Themes: _____

Rating: ⭐ ⭐ ⭐ ⭐ ⭐ Characters: _____

Steam Level: 🌶 🌶 🌶 🌶 🌶 Book Type: Book | Ebook | Audio

Recommend: Y ☐ N ☐ To: _____

Summary

What I Loved

Quotes to Keep

66

99

Book Review

Title: _____ Author: _____

Published Date: _____ Series: _____

Category: _____ Trope: _____

Date Read: _____ Themes: _____

Rating: ⭐ ⭐ ⭐ ⭐ ⭐ Characters: _____

Steam Level: 🌶 🌶 🌶 🌶 🌶 Book Type: Book | Ebook | Audio

Recommend: Y ☐ N ☐ To: _____

Summary

What I Loved

Quotes to Keep

"

"

Book Review

Title: _____   Author: _____

Published Date: _____   Series: _____

Category: _____   Trope: _____

Date Read: _____   Themes: _____

Rating: ⭐ ⭐ ⭐ ⭐ ⭐   Characters: _____

Steam Level: 🌶 🌶 🌶 🌶 🌶   Book Type: Book | Ebook | Audio

Recommend: Y ☐ N ☐   To: _____

Summary

What I Loved

Quotes to Keep

66

99

Book Review

Title: _____   Author: _____

Published Date: _____   Series: _____

Category: _____   Trope: _____

Date Read: _____   Themes: _____

Rating: ⭐ ⭐ ⭐ ⭐ ⭐   Characters: _____

Steam Level: 🌶️ 🌶️ 🌶️ 🌶️ 🌶️   Book Type: Book | Ebook | Audio

Recommend: Y ☐   N ☐   To: _____

Summary

What I Loved

Quotes to Keep

66

99

Book Review

Title: _____   Author: _____

Published Date: _____   Series: _____

Category: _____   Trope: _____

Date Read: _____   Themes: _____

Rating: ⭐ ⭐ ⭐ ⭐ ⭐   Characters: _____

Steam Level: 🌶 🌶 🌶 🌶 🌶   Book Type: Book | Ebook | Audio

Recommend: Y ☐   N ☐   To: _____

Summary

What I Loved

Quotes to Keep

"

"

Book Review

Title: _____   Author: _____

Published Date: _____   Series: _____

Category: _____   Trope: _____

Date Read: _____   Themes: _____

Rating: ⭐ ⭐ ⭐ ⭐ ⭐   Characters: _____

Steam Level: 🌶 🌶 🌶 🌶 🌶   Book Type: Book | Ebook | Audio

Recommend: Y ☐   N ☐   To: _____

Summary

What I Loved

Quotes to Keep

66

99

Book Review

Title: _____ Author: _____

Published Date: _____ Series: _____

Category: _____ Trope: _____

Date Read: _____ Themes: _____

Rating: ⭐ ⭐ ⭐ ⭐ ⭐ Characters: _____

Steam Level: 🌶 🌶 🌶 🌶 🌶 Book Type: Book | Ebook | Audio

Recommend: Y ☐ N ☐ To: _____

Summary

What I Loved

Quotes to Keep

66

99

Book Review

Title: _____ Author: _____

Published Date: _____ Series: _____

Category: _____ Trope: _____

Date Read: _____ Themes: _____

Rating: ⭐ ⭐ ⭐ ⭐ ⭐ Characters: _____

Steam Level: 🌶 🌶 🌶 🌶 🌶 Book Type: Book | Ebook | Audio

Recommend: Y ☐   N ☐   To: _____

Summary

What I Loved

Quotes to Keep

"

"

Book Review

Title: _____

Author: _____

Published Date: _____

Series: _____

Category: _____

Trope: _____

Date Read: _____

Themes: _____

Rating: ⭐ ⭐ ⭐ ⭐ ⭐

Characters: _____

Steam Level: 🌶 🌶 🌶 🌶 🌶

Book Type: Book | Ebook | Audio

Recommend: Y ☐   N ☐   To: _____

Summary

What I Loved

Quotes to Keep

"

"

Book Review

Title: _____   Author: _____

Published Date: _____   Series: _____

Category: _____   Trope: _____

Date Read: _____   Themes: _____

Rating: ⭐ ⭐ ⭐ ⭐ ⭐   Characters: _____

Steam Level: 🌶 🌶 🌶 🌶 🌶   Book Type: Book | Ebook | Audio

Recommend: Y ☐   N ☐   To: _____

Summary

What I Loved

Quotes to Keep

66

99

Book Review

Title: _____   Author: _____

Published Date: _____   Series: _____

Category: _____   Trope: _____

Date Read: _____   Themes: _____

Rating: ⭐ ⭐ ⭐ ⭐ ⭐   Characters: _____

Steam Level: 🌶 🌶 🌶 🌶 🌶   Book Type: Book | Ebook | Audio

Recommend: Y ☐ N ☐ To: _____

Summary

What I Loved

Quotes to Keep

66

99

Book Review

Title: _____   Author: _____

Published Date: _____   Series: _____

Category: _____   Trope: _____

Date Read: _____   Themes: _____

Rating: ⭐ ⭐ ⭐ ⭐ ⭐   Characters: _____

Steam Level: 🌶 🌶 🌶 🌶 🌶   Book Type: Book | Ebook | Audio

Recommend: Y ☐   N ☐   To: _____

Summary

What I Loved

Quotes to Keep

66

99

Book Review

Title: _____ Author: _____

Published Date: _____ Series: _____

Category: _____ Trope: _____

Date Read: _____ Themes: _____

Rating: ⭐ ⭐ ⭐ ⭐ ⭐ Characters: _____

Steam Level: 🌶 🌶 🌶 🌶 🌶 Book Type: Book | Ebook | Audio

Recommend: Y ☐   N ☐   To: _____

Summary

What I Loved

Quotes to Keep

66

99

Book Review

Title: _____   Author: _____

Published Date: _____   Series: _____

Category: _____   Trope: _____

Date Read: _____   Themes: _____

Rating: ⭐ ⭐ ⭐ ⭐ ⭐   Characters: _____

Steam Level: 🌶 🌶 🌶 🌶 🌶   Book Type: Book | Ebook | Audio

Recommend: Y ☐   N ☐   To: _____

Summary

What I Loved

Quotes to Keep

66

99

Book Review

Title: _____ Author: _____

Published Date: _____ Series: _____

Category: _____ Trope: _____

Date Read: _____ Themes: _____

Rating: ⭐ ⭐ ⭐ ⭐ ⭐ Characters: _____

Steam Level: 🌶 🌶 🌶 🌶 🌶 Book Type: Book | Ebook | Audio

Recommend: Y ☐   N ☐   To: _____

Summary

What I Loved

Quotes to Keep

66

99

Book Review

Title: _____   Author: _____

Published Date: _____   Series: _____

Category: _____   Trope: _____

Date Read: _____   Themes: _____

Rating: ⭐ ⭐ ⭐ ⭐ ⭐   Characters: _____

Steam Level: 🌶 🌶 🌶 🌶 🌶   Book Type: Book | Ebook | Audio

Recommend: Y ☐   N ☐   To: _____

Summary

What I Loved

Quotes to Keep

"

"

Book Review

Title: _____ Author: _____

Published Date: _____ Series: _____

Category: _____ Trope: _____

Date Read: _____ Themes: _____

Rating: ⭐ ⭐ ⭐ ⭐ ⭐ Characters: _____

Steam Level: 🌶 🌶 🌶 🌶 🌶 Book Type: Book | Ebook | Audio

Recommend: Y ☐ N ☐ To: _____

Summary

What I Loved

Quotes to Keep

66

99

Book Review

Title: _____   Author: _____

Published Date: _____   Series: _____

Category: _____   Trope: _____

Date Read: _____   Themes: _____

Rating: ⭐ ⭐ ⭐ ⭐ ⭐   Characters: _____

Steam Level: 🌶 🌶 🌶 🌶 🌶   Book Type: Book | Ebook | Audio

Recommend: Y ☐   N ☐   To: _____

What I Loved

Quotes to Keep

"

"

Book Review

Title: _____   Author: _____

Published Date: _____   Series: _____

Category: _____   Trope: _____

Date Read: _____   Themes: _____

Rating: ⭐ ⭐ ⭐ ⭐ ⭐   Characters: _____

Steam Level: 🌶 🌶 🌶 🌶 🌶   Book Type: Book | Ebook | Audio

Recommend: Y ☐   N ☐   To: _____

Summary

What I Loved

Quotes to Keep

66

99

Book Review

Title: _____ Author: _____

Published Date: _____ Series: _____

Category: _____ Trope: _____

Date Read: _____ Themes: _____

Rating: ⭐ ⭐ ⭐ ⭐ ⭐ Characters: _____

Steam Level: 🌶 🌶 🌶 🌶 🌶 Book Type: Book | Ebook | Audio

Recommend: Y ☐   N ☐   To: _____

Summary

What I Loved

Quotes to Keep

66

99

Book Review

Title: _____

Author: _____

Published Date: _____

Series: _____

Category: _____

Trope: _____

Date Read: _____

Themes: _____

Rating: ★ ★ ★ ★ ★

Characters: _____

Steam Level: 🌶 🌶 🌶 🌶 🌶

Book Type: Book | Ebook | Audio

Recommend: Y ☐   N ☐   To: _____

Summary

What I Loved

Quotes to Keep

66

99

Book Review

Title: _____ Author: _____

Published Date: _____ Series: _____

Category: _____ Trope: _____

Date Read: _____ Themes: _____

Rating: ⭐ ⭐ ⭐ ⭐ ⭐   Characters: _____

Steam Level: 🌶 🌶 🌶 🌶 🌶   Book Type: Book | Ebook | Audio

Recommend: Y ☐ N ☐ To: _____

Summary

What I Loved

Quotes to Keep

66

99

Book Review

Title: _____   Author: _____

Published Date: _____   Series: _____

Category: _____   Trope: _____

Date Read: _____   Themes: _____

Rating: ⭐ ⭐ ⭐ ⭐ ⭐   Characters: _____

Steam Level: 🌶 🌶 🌶 🌶 🌶   Book Type: Book | Ebook | Audio

Recommend: Y ☐   N ☐   To: _____

Summary

What I Loved

Quotes to Keep

"

"

Book Review

Title: _____   Author: _____

Published Date: _____   Series: _____

Category: _____   Trope: _____

Date Read: _____   Themes: _____

Rating: ⭐ ⭐ ⭐ ⭐ ⭐   Characters: _____

Steam Level: 🌶 🌶 🌶 🌶 🌶   Book Type: Book | Ebook | Audio

Recommend: Y ☐ N ☐ To: _____

Summary

What I Loved

Quotes to Keep

66

99

Book Review

Title: _____ Author: _____

Published Date: _____ Series: _____

Category: _____ Trope: _____

Date Read: _____ Themes: _____

Rating: ⭐ ⭐ ⭐ ⭐ ⭐ Characters: _____

Steam Level: 🌶 🌶 🌶 🌶 🌶 Book Type: Book | Ebook | Audio

Recommend: Y ☐ N ☐ To: _____

Summary

What I Loved

Quotes to Keep

"

"

Book Review

Title: _____ Author: _____

Published Date: _____ Series: _____

Category: _____ Trope: _____

Date Read: _____ Themes: _____

Rating: ⭐ ⭐ ⭐ ⭐ ⭐ Characters: _____

Steam Level: 🌶 🌶 🌶 🌶 🌶 Book Type: Book | Ebook | Audio

Recommend: Y ☐ N ☐ To: _____

Summary

What I Loved

Quotes to Keep

66

99

Book Review

Title: _____   Author: _____

Published Date: _____   Series: _____

Category: _____   Trope: _____

Date Read: _____   Themes: _____

Rating: ⭐ ⭐ ⭐ ⭐ ⭐   Characters: _____

Steam Level: 🌶 🌶 🌶 🌶 🌶   Book Type: Book | Ebook | Audio

Recommend: Y ☐   N ☐   To: _____

Summary

What I Loved

Quotes to Keep

66

99

Book Review

Title: _____   Author: _____

Published Date: _____   Series: _____

Category: _____   Trope: _____

Date Read: _____   Themes: _____

Rating: ⭐ ⭐ ⭐ ⭐ ⭐   Characters: _____

Steam Level: 🌶 🌶 🌶 🌶 🌶   Book Type: Book | Ebook | Audio

Recommend: Y ☐   N ☐   To: _____

Summary

What I Loved

Quotes to Keep

"

"

Book Review

Title: _____   Author: _____

Published Date: _____   Series: _____

Category: _____   Trope: _____

Date Read: _____   Themes: _____

Rating: ⭐ ⭐ ⭐ ⭐ ⭐   Characters: _____

Steam Level: 🌶 🌶 🌶 🌶 🌶   Book Type: Book | Ebook | Audio

Recommend: Y ☐   N ☐   To: _____

Summary

What I Loved

Quotes to Keep

❝

❞

Book Review

Title: _____   Author: _____

Published Date: _____   Series: _____

Category: _____   Trope: _____

Date Read: _____   Themes: _____

Rating: ⭐ ⭐ ⭐ ⭐ ⭐   Characters: _____

Steam Level: 🌶 🌶 🌶 🌶 🌶   Book Type: Book | Ebook | Audio

Recommend: Y ☐   N ☐   To: _____

Summary

What I Loved

Quotes to Keep

66

99

Book Review

Title: _____ Author: _____

Published Date: _____ Series: _____

Category: _____ Trope: _____

Date Read: _____ Themes: _____

Rating: ⭐ ⭐ ⭐ ⭐ ⭐   Characters: _____

Steam Level: 🌶 🌶 🌶 🌶 🌶   Book Type: Book | Ebook | Audio

Recommend: Y ☐ N ☐ To: _____

Summary

What I Loved

Quotes to Keep

66

99

Book Review

Title: _____ Author: _____

Published Date: _____ Series: _____

Category: _____ Trope: _____

Date Read: _____ Themes: _____

Rating: ⭐ ⭐ ⭐ ⭐ ⭐ Characters: _____

Steam Level: 🌶 🌶 🌶 🌶 🌶 Book Type: Book | Ebook | Audio

Recommend: Y ☐ N ☐ To: _____

Summary

What I Loved

Quotes to Keep

66

99

Book Review

Title: _____   Author: _____

Published Date: _____   Series: _____

Category: _____   Trope: _____

Date Read: _____   Themes: _____

Rating: ⭐ ⭐ ⭐ ⭐ ⭐   Characters: _____

Steam Level: 🌶 🌶 🌶 🌶 🌶   Book Type: Book | Ebook | Audio

Recommend: Y ☐   N ☐   To: _____

Summary

What I Loved

Quotes to Keep

66

99

Book Review

Title: _____ Author: _____

Published Date: _____ Series: _____

Category: _____ Trope: _____

Date Read: _____ Themes: _____

Rating: ⭐ ⭐ ⭐ ⭐ ⭐   Characters: _____

Steam Level: 🌶 🌶 🌶 🌶 🌶   Book Type: Book | Ebook | Audio

Recommend: Y ☐   N ☐   To: _____

Summary

What I Loved

Quotes to Keep

66

99

Book Review

Title: _____   Author: _____

Published Date: _____   Series: _____

Category: _____   Trope: _____

Date Read: _____   Themes: _____

Rating: ⭐ ⭐ ⭐ ⭐ ⭐   Characters: _____

Steam Level: 🌶 🌶 🌶 🌶 🌶   Book Type: Book | Ebook | Audio

Recommend: Y ☐   N ☐   To: _____

Summary

What I Loved

Quotes to Keep

66

99

Book Review

Title: _____ Author: _____

Published Date: _____ Series: _____

Category: _____ Trope: _____

Date Read: _____ Themes: _____

Rating: ⭐ ⭐ ⭐ ⭐ ⭐ Characters: _____

Steam Level: 🌶 🌶 🌶 🌶 🌶 Book Type: Book | Ebook | Audio

Recommend: Y ☐ N ☐ To: _____

Summary

What I Loved

Quotes to Keep

" "

Book Review

Title: _____ Author: _____

Published Date: _____ Series: _____

Category: _____ Trope: _____

Date Read: _____ Themes: _____

Rating: ⭐ ⭐ ⭐ ⭐ ⭐   Characters: _____

Steam Level: 🌶 🌶 🌶 🌶 🌶   Book Type: Book | Ebook | Audio

Recommend: Y ☐ N ☐ To: _____

Summary

What I Loved

Quotes to Keep

66

99

Book Review

Title: _____   Author: _____

Published Date: _____   Series: _____

Category: _____   Trope: _____

Date Read: _____   Themes: _____

Rating: ⭐ ⭐ ⭐ ⭐ ⭐   Characters: _____

Steam Level: 🌶 🌶 🌶 🌶 🌶   Book Type: Book | Ebook | Audio

Recommend: Y ☐   N ☐   To: _____

Summary

What I Loved

Quotes to Keep

66

99

Book Review

Title: _____ Author: _____

Published Date: _____ Series: _____

Category: _____ Trope: _____

Date Read: _____ Themes: _____

Rating: ⭐ ⭐ ⭐ ⭐ ⭐ Characters: _____

Steam Level: 🌶 🌶 🌶 🌶 🌶 Book Type: Book | Ebook | Audio

Recommend: Y ☐ N ☐ To: _____

Summary

What I Loved

Quotes to Keep

66

99

Book Review

Title: _____   Author: _____

Published Date: _____   Series: _____

Category: _____   Trope: _____

Date Read: _____   Themes: _____

Rating: ⭐ ⭐ ⭐ ⭐ ⭐   Characters: _____

Steam Level: 🌶 🌶 🌶 🌶 🌶   Book Type: Book | Ebook | Audio

Recommend: Y ☐   N ☐   To: _____

Summary

What I Loved

Quotes to Keep

66

99

Book Review

Title: _____ Author: _____

Published Date: _____ Series: _____

Category: _____ Trope: _____

Date Read: _____ Themes: _____

Rating: ⭐ ⭐ ⭐ ⭐ ⭐ Characters: _____

Steam Level: 🌶 🌶 🌶 🌶 🌶 Book Type: Book | Ebook | Audio

Recommend: Y ☐ N ☐ To: _____

Summary

What I Loved

Quotes to Keep

66

99

Book Review

Title: _____   Author: _____

Published Date: _____   Series: _____

Category: _____   Trope: _____

Date Read: _____   Themes: _____

Rating: ⭐ ⭐ ⭐ ⭐ ⭐   Characters: _____

Steam Level: 🌶 🌶 🌶 🌶 🌶   Book Type: Book | Ebook | Audio

Recommend: Y ☐   N ☐   To: _____

What I Loved

Quotes to Keep

66

99

Book Review

Title: _____   Author: _____

Published Date: _____   Series: _____

Category: _____   Trope: _____

Date Read: _____   Themes: _____

Rating: ⭐ ⭐ ⭐ ⭐ ⭐   Characters: _____

Steam Level: 🌶 🌶 🌶 🌶 🌶   Book Type: Book | Ebook | Audio

Recommend: Y ☐   N ☐   To: _____

Summary

What I Loved

Quotes to Keep

"

"

Book Review

Title: _____ Author: _____

Published Date: _____ Series: _____

Category: _____ Trope: _____

Date Read: _____ Themes: _____

Rating: ⭐ ⭐ ⭐ ⭐ ⭐ Characters: _____

Steam Level: 🌶 🌶 🌶 🌶 🌶 Book Type: Book | Ebook | Audio

Recommend: Y ☐ N ☐ To: _____

Summary

What I Loved

Quotes to Keep

❝

❞

Book Review

Title: _____

Author: _____

Published Date: _____

Series: _____

Category: _____

Trope: _____

Date Read: _____

Themes: _____

Rating: ⭐ ⭐ ⭐ ⭐ ⭐

Characters: _____

Steam Level: 🌶 🌶 🌶 🌶 🌶

Book Type: Book | Ebook | Audio

Recommend: Y ☐   N ☐   To: _____

Summary

What I Loved

Quotes to Keep

66

99

Book Review

Title: _____ Author: _____

Published Date: _____ Series: _____

Category: _____ Trope: _____

Date Read: _____ Themes: _____

Rating: ⭐ ⭐ ⭐ ⭐ ⭐ Characters: _____

Steam Level: 🌶 🌶 🌶 🌶 🌶 Book Type: Book | Ebook | Audio

Recommend: Y ☐ N ☐ To: _____

Summary

What I Loved

Quotes to Keep

" "

Book Review

Title: _____

Author: _____

Published Date: _____

Series: _____

Category: _____

Trope: _____

Date Read: _____

Themes: _____

Rating: ⭐ ⭐ ⭐ ⭐ ⭐

Characters: _____

Steam Level: 🌶 🌶 🌶 🌶 🌶

Book Type: Book | Ebook | Audio

Recommend: Y ☐   N ☐   To: _____

Summary

What I Loved

Quotes to Keep

66

99

Book Review

Title: _____   Author: _____

Published Date: _____   Series: _____

Category: _____   Trope: _____

Date Read: _____   Themes: _____

Rating: ⭐ ⭐ ⭐ ⭐ ⭐   Characters: _____

Steam Level: 🌶 🌶 🌶 🌶 🌶   Book Type: Book | Ebook | Audio

Recommend: Y ☐   N ☐   To: _____

Summary

What I Loved

Quotes to Keep

"

„

Book Review

Title: _____   Author: _____

Published Date: _____   Series: _____

Category: _____   Trope: _____

Date Read: _____   Themes: _____

Rating: ⭐ ⭐ ⭐ ⭐ ⭐   Characters: _____

Steam Level: 🌶 🌶 🌶 🌶 🌶   Book Type: Book | Ebook | Audio

Recommend: Y ☐ N ☐ To: _____

Summary

What I Loved

Quotes to Keep

66

99

Book Review

Title: _____ Author: _____

Published Date: _____ Series: _____

Category: _____ Trope: _____

Date Read: _____ Themes: _____

Rating: ⭐ ⭐ ⭐ ⭐ ⭐ Characters: _____

Steam Level: 🌶 🌶 🌶 🌶 🌶 Book Type: Book | Ebook | Audio

Recommend: Y ☐   N ☐   To: _____

Summary

What I Loved

Quotes to Keep

"

"

Book Review

Title: _____   Author: _____

Published Date: _____   Series: _____

Category: _____   Trope: _____

Date Read: _____   Themes: _____

Rating: ⭐ ⭐ ⭐ ⭐ ⭐   Characters: _____

Steam Level: 🌶 🌶 🌶 🌶 🌶   Book Type: Book | Ebook | Audio

Recommend: Y ☐   N ☐   To: _____

Summary

What I Loved

Quotes to Keep

66

99

Book Series Review

Series: _____   Author: _____

First Published: _____   Last Published: _____

BOOK 1
Title:
Thoughts:

Date Published:
Trope:

Rating: ⭐ ⭐ ⭐ ⭐ ⭐

BOOK 2
Title:
Thoughts:

Date Published:
Trope:

Rating: ⭐ ⭐ ⭐ ⭐ ⭐

BOOK 3
Title:
Thoughts:

Date Published:
Trope:

Rating: ⭐ ⭐ ⭐ ⭐ ⭐

BOOK 4
Title:
Thoughts:

Date Published:
Trope:

Rating: ⭐ ⭐ ⭐ ⭐ ⭐

BOOK 5
Title:
Thoughts:

Date Published:
Trope:

Rating: ⭐ ⭐ ⭐ ⭐ ⭐

Book Series Review

Series: _____   Author: _____

First Published: _____   Last Published: _____

BOOK 1
Title:
Thoughts:

Date Published:
Trope:

Rating: ★ ★ ★ ★ ★

BOOK 2
Title:
Thoughts:

Date Published:
Trope:

Rating: ★ ★ ★ ★ ★

BOOK 3
Title:
Thoughts:

Date Published:
Trope:

Rating: ★ ★ ★ ★ ★

BOOK 4
Title:
Thoughts:

Date Published:
Trope:

Rating: ★ ★ ★ ★ ★

BOOK 5
Title:
Thoughts:

Date Published:
Trope:

Rating: ★ ★ ★ ★ ★

Book Series Review

Series: _____   Author: _____

First Published: _____   Last Published: _____

BOOK 1
Title:
Thoughts:

Date Published:
Trope:

Rating: ☆ ☆ ☆ ☆ ☆

BOOK 2
Title:
Thoughts:

Date Published:
Trope:

Rating: ☆ ☆ ☆ ☆ ☆

BOOK 3
Title:
Thoughts:

Date Published:
Trope:

Rating: ☆ ☆ ☆ ☆ ☆

BOOK 4
Title:
Thoughts:

Date Published:
Trope:

Rating: ☆ ☆ ☆ ☆ ☆

BOOK 5
Title:
Thoughts:

Date Published:
Trope:

Rating: ☆ ☆ ☆ ☆ ☆

Book
Categories
& Tropes

Billionaire Romance Books

Title	Author	Rating
		☆ ☆ ☆ ☆ ☆
		☆ ☆ ☆ ☆ ☆
		☆ ☆ ☆ ☆ ☆
		☆ ☆ ☆ ☆ ☆
		☆ ☆ ☆ ☆ ☆
		☆ ☆ ☆ ☆ ☆
		☆ ☆ ☆ ☆ ☆
		☆ ☆ ☆ ☆ ☆
		☆ ☆ ☆ ☆ ☆
		☆ ☆ ☆ ☆ ☆
		☆ ☆ ☆ ☆ ☆
		☆ ☆ ☆ ☆ ☆
		☆ ☆ ☆ ☆ ☆

College Romance Books

Title	Author	Rating
		☆ ☆ ☆ ☆ ☆
		☆ ☆ ☆ ☆ ☆
		☆ ☆ ☆ ☆ ☆
		☆ ☆ ☆ ☆ ☆
		☆ ☆ ☆ ☆ ☆
		☆ ☆ ☆ ☆ ☆
		☆ ☆ ☆ ☆ ☆
		☆ ☆ ☆ ☆ ☆
		☆ ☆ ☆ ☆ ☆
		☆ ☆ ☆ ☆ ☆
		☆ ☆ ☆ ☆ ☆
		☆ ☆ ☆ ☆ ☆
		☆ ☆ ☆ ☆ ☆

Enemies to Lovers Romance Books

Title	Author	Rating
		☆ ☆ ☆ ☆ ☆
		☆ ☆ ☆ ☆ ☆
		☆ ☆ ☆ ☆ ☆
		☆ ☆ ☆ ☆ ☆
		☆ ☆ ☆ ☆ ☆
		☆ ☆ ☆ ☆ ☆
		☆ ☆ ☆ ☆ ☆
		☆ ☆ ☆ ☆ ☆
		☆ ☆ ☆ ☆ ☆
		☆ ☆ ☆ ☆ ☆
		☆ ☆ ☆ ☆ ☆
		☆ ☆ ☆ ☆ ☆

Erotic Romance Books

Title	Author	Rating
		☆ ☆ ☆ ☆ ☆
		☆ ☆ ☆ ☆ ☆
		☆ ☆ ☆ ☆ ☆
		☆ ☆ ☆ ☆ ☆
		☆ ☆ ☆ ☆ ☆
		☆ ☆ ☆ ☆ ☆
		☆ ☆ ☆ ☆ ☆
		☆ ☆ ☆ ☆ ☆
		☆ ☆ ☆ ☆ ☆
		☆ ☆ ☆ ☆ ☆
		☆ ☆ ☆ ☆ ☆
		☆ ☆ ☆ ☆ ☆
		☆ ☆ ☆ ☆ ☆

Fake Relationship Romance Books

Title	Author	Rating
		☆ ☆ ☆ ☆ ☆
		☆ ☆ ☆ ☆ ☆
		☆ ☆ ☆ ☆ ☆
		☆ ☆ ☆ ☆ ☆
		☆ ☆ ☆ ☆ ☆
		☆ ☆ ☆ ☆ ☆
		☆ ☆ ☆ ☆ ☆
		☆ ☆ ☆ ☆ ☆
		☆ ☆ ☆ ☆ ☆
		☆ ☆ ☆ ☆ ☆
		☆ ☆ ☆ ☆ ☆
		☆ ☆ ☆ ☆ ☆
		☆ ☆ ☆ ☆ ☆

Fantasy Romance Books

Title	Author	Rating
		☆ ☆ ☆ ☆ ☆
		☆ ☆ ☆ ☆ ☆
		☆ ☆ ☆ ☆ ☆
		☆ ☆ ☆ ☆ ☆
		☆ ☆ ☆ ☆ ☆
		☆ ☆ ☆ ☆ ☆
		☆ ☆ ☆ ☆ ☆
		☆ ☆ ☆ ☆ ☆
		☆ ☆ ☆ ☆ ☆
		☆ ☆ ☆ ☆ ☆
		☆ ☆ ☆ ☆ ☆
		☆ ☆ ☆ ☆ ☆
		☆ ☆ ☆ ☆ ☆

Forced Proximity Romance Books

Title	Author	Rating
		☆☆☆☆☆
		☆☆☆☆☆
		☆☆☆☆☆
		☆☆☆☆☆
		☆☆☆☆☆
		☆☆☆☆☆
		☆☆☆☆☆
		☆☆☆☆☆
		☆☆☆☆☆
		☆☆☆☆☆
		☆☆☆☆☆
		☆☆☆☆☆
		☆☆☆☆☆

Friends to Lovers Romance Books

Title	Author	Rating
		☆ ☆ ☆ ☆ ☆
		☆ ☆ ☆ ☆ ☆
		☆ ☆ ☆ ☆ ☆
		☆ ☆ ☆ ☆ ☆
		☆ ☆ ☆ ☆ ☆
		☆ ☆ ☆ ☆ ☆
		☆ ☆ ☆ ☆ ☆
		☆ ☆ ☆ ☆ ☆
		☆ ☆ ☆ ☆ ☆
		☆ ☆ ☆ ☆ ☆
		☆ ☆ ☆ ☆ ☆
		☆ ☆ ☆ ☆ ☆
		☆ ☆ ☆ ☆ ☆

Historical Romance Books

Title	Author	Rating
		☆ ☆ ☆ ☆ ☆
		☆ ☆ ☆ ☆ ☆
		☆ ☆ ☆ ☆ ☆
		☆ ☆ ☆ ☆ ☆
		☆ ☆ ☆ ☆ ☆
		☆ ☆ ☆ ☆ ☆
		☆ ☆ ☆ ☆ ☆
		☆ ☆ ☆ ☆ ☆
		☆ ☆ ☆ ☆ ☆
		☆ ☆ ☆ ☆ ☆
		☆ ☆ ☆ ☆ ☆
		☆ ☆ ☆ ☆ ☆
		☆ ☆ ☆ ☆ ☆

Lesbian/Sapphic Romance Books

Title	Author	Rating
		☆☆☆☆☆
		☆☆☆☆☆
		☆☆☆☆☆
		☆☆☆☆☆
		☆☆☆☆☆
		☆☆☆☆☆
		☆☆☆☆☆
		☆☆☆☆☆
		☆☆☆☆☆
		☆☆☆☆☆
		☆☆☆☆☆
		☆☆☆☆☆
		☆☆☆☆☆

Mafia Romance Books

Title	Author	Rating
		☆ ☆ ☆ ☆ ☆
		☆ ☆ ☆ ☆ ☆
		☆ ☆ ☆ ☆ ☆
		☆ ☆ ☆ ☆ ☆
		☆ ☆ ☆ ☆ ☆
		☆ ☆ ☆ ☆ ☆
		☆ ☆ ☆ ☆ ☆
		☆ ☆ ☆ ☆ ☆
		☆ ☆ ☆ ☆ ☆
		☆ ☆ ☆ ☆ ☆
		☆ ☆ ☆ ☆ ☆
		☆ ☆ ☆ ☆ ☆
		☆ ☆ ☆ ☆ ☆

MM Romance Books

Title	Author	Rating
		☆ ☆ ☆ ☆ ☆
		☆ ☆ ☆ ☆ ☆
		☆ ☆ ☆ ☆ ☆
		☆ ☆ ☆ ☆ ☆
		☆ ☆ ☆ ☆ ☆
		☆ ☆ ☆ ☆ ☆
		☆ ☆ ☆ ☆ ☆
		☆ ☆ ☆ ☆ ☆
		☆ ☆ ☆ ☆ ☆
		☆ ☆ ☆ ☆ ☆
		☆ ☆ ☆ ☆ ☆
		☆ ☆ ☆ ☆ ☆
		☆ ☆ ☆ ☆ ☆

New Adult Romance Books

Title	Author	Rating
		☆ ☆ ☆ ☆ ☆
		☆ ☆ ☆ ☆ ☆
		☆ ☆ ☆ ☆ ☆
		☆ ☆ ☆ ☆ ☆
		☆ ☆ ☆ ☆ ☆
		☆ ☆ ☆ ☆ ☆
		☆ ☆ ☆ ☆ ☆
		☆ ☆ ☆ ☆ ☆
		☆ ☆ ☆ ☆ ☆
		☆ ☆ ☆ ☆ ☆
		☆ ☆ ☆ ☆ ☆
		☆ ☆ ☆ ☆ ☆
		☆ ☆ ☆ ☆ ☆

Paranormal Romance Books

Title	Author	Rating
		☆ ☆ ☆ ☆ ☆
		☆ ☆ ☆ ☆ ☆
		☆ ☆ ☆ ☆ ☆
		☆ ☆ ☆ ☆ ☆
		☆ ☆ ☆ ☆ ☆
		☆ ☆ ☆ ☆ ☆
		☆ ☆ ☆ ☆ ☆
		☆ ☆ ☆ ☆ ☆
		☆ ☆ ☆ ☆ ☆
		☆ ☆ ☆ ☆ ☆
		☆ ☆ ☆ ☆ ☆
		☆ ☆ ☆ ☆ ☆

Second Chance Romance Books

Title	Author	Rating
		☆ ☆ ☆ ☆ ☆
		☆ ☆ ☆ ☆ ☆
		☆ ☆ ☆ ☆ ☆
		☆ ☆ ☆ ☆ ☆
		☆ ☆ ☆ ☆ ☆
		☆ ☆ ☆ ☆ ☆
		☆ ☆ ☆ ☆ ☆
		☆ ☆ ☆ ☆ ☆
		☆ ☆ ☆ ☆ ☆
		☆ ☆ ☆ ☆ ☆
		☆ ☆ ☆ ☆ ☆
		☆ ☆ ☆ ☆ ☆
		☆ ☆ ☆ ☆ ☆

Slow Burn Romance Books

Title	Author	Rating
		☆ ☆ ☆ ☆ ☆
		☆ ☆ ☆ ☆ ☆
		☆ ☆ ☆ ☆ ☆
		☆ ☆ ☆ ☆ ☆
		☆ ☆ ☆ ☆ ☆
		☆ ☆ ☆ ☆ ☆
		☆ ☆ ☆ ☆ ☆
		☆ ☆ ☆ ☆ ☆
		☆ ☆ ☆ ☆ ☆
		☆ ☆ ☆ ☆ ☆
		☆ ☆ ☆ ☆ ☆
		☆ ☆ ☆ ☆ ☆
		☆ ☆ ☆ ☆ ☆

Sports Romance Books

Title	Author	Rating
		☆ ☆ ☆ ☆ ☆
		☆ ☆ ☆ ☆ ☆
		☆ ☆ ☆ ☆ ☆
		☆ ☆ ☆ ☆ ☆
		☆ ☆ ☆ ☆ ☆
		☆ ☆ ☆ ☆ ☆
		☆ ☆ ☆ ☆ ☆
		☆ ☆ ☆ ☆ ☆
		☆ ☆ ☆ ☆ ☆
		☆ ☆ ☆ ☆ ☆
		☆ ☆ ☆ ☆ ☆
		☆ ☆ ☆ ☆ ☆
		☆ ☆ ☆ ☆ ☆

Young Adult Romance Books

Title	Author	Rating
		☆ ☆ ☆ ☆ ☆
		☆ ☆ ☆ ☆ ☆
		☆ ☆ ☆ ☆ ☆
		☆ ☆ ☆ ☆ ☆
		☆ ☆ ☆ ☆ ☆
		☆ ☆ ☆ ☆ ☆
		☆ ☆ ☆ ☆ ☆
		☆ ☆ ☆ ☆ ☆
		☆ ☆ ☆ ☆ ☆
		☆ ☆ ☆ ☆ ☆
		☆ ☆ ☆ ☆ ☆
		☆ ☆ ☆ ☆ ☆
		☆ ☆ ☆ ☆ ☆

Title	Author	Rating
		☆ ☆ ☆ ☆ ☆
		☆ ☆ ☆ ☆ ☆
		☆ ☆ ☆ ☆ ☆
		☆ ☆ ☆ ☆ ☆
		☆ ☆ ☆ ☆ ☆
		☆ ☆ ☆ ☆ ☆
		☆ ☆ ☆ ☆ ☆
		☆ ☆ ☆ ☆ ☆
		☆ ☆ ☆ ☆ ☆
		☆ ☆ ☆ ☆ ☆
		☆ ☆ ☆ ☆ ☆
		☆ ☆ ☆ ☆ ☆

Title	Author	Rating
		☆☆☆☆☆
		☆☆☆☆☆
		☆☆☆☆☆
		☆☆☆☆☆
		☆☆☆☆☆
		☆☆☆☆☆
		☆☆☆☆☆
		☆☆☆☆☆
		☆☆☆☆☆
		☆☆☆☆☆
		☆☆☆☆☆
		☆☆☆☆☆
		☆☆☆☆☆

Title	Author	Rating
		☆ ☆ ☆ ☆ ☆
		☆ ☆ ☆ ☆ ☆
		☆ ☆ ☆ ☆ ☆
		☆ ☆ ☆ ☆ ☆
		☆ ☆ ☆ ☆ ☆
		☆ ☆ ☆ ☆ ☆
		☆ ☆ ☆ ☆ ☆
		☆ ☆ ☆ ☆ ☆
		☆ ☆ ☆ ☆ ☆
		☆ ☆ ☆ ☆ ☆
		☆ ☆ ☆ ☆ ☆
		☆ ☆ ☆ ☆ ☆

Reading Year in Review

of Books I Wanted to Read: _____   # of Books I Read: _____

book: _____   ebook: _____   audio: _____

_____ contemporary   _____ erotic   _____ romantic suspense

_____ historical   _____ sports   _____ romantic comedy

_____ new adult   _____ fantasy   _____ dark romance

_____ young adult   _____ paranormal   _____ novella

Top 10 Favorites:

_____

_____

_____

_____

_____

_____

_____

_____

_____

_____

Books to Read Next Year:

_____

_____

_____

New Authors I Read:

_____

_____

Things I've Learned
Reading Romance

Things I've Learned
Reading Romance

Notes | Reflections | Doodles

66

Life is better
with a love story

-Leslie

She Reads Romance Books

Printed in Great Britain
by Amazon

14451524R00092